# I WANT TO TELL YOU HOW I FEEL, HOW I FEEL, GOD

## GORDON BAILEY

A LION PAPERBACK

Copyright © 1983 Gordon Bailey

Published by
**Lion Publishing**
Icknield Way, Tring, Herts, England
ISBN 0 85648 339 7
**Albatross Books**
PO Box 320, Sutherland, NSW 2232, Australia
ISBN 0 86760 385 2

First edition 1983

Photographs by
Barnabys Picture Library, 39
Robin Bath, facing foreword
Sylvester Jacobs, 33, 73
Lion Publishing/David Alexander, 25;
Paul Crooks, 53; Jon Willcocks, 15, 20,
28, 47, 59, 67

Printed and bound in Great Britain by
Blantyre Printing and Binding Company Ltd, Glasgow

# I want to tell you how I feel, God

O God, I feel rotten.
You know what I did,
and you know how lousy it's making me feel;
I didn't think I had much of a conscience,
till now.
You'd think feelings as bad as this
would stop me doing wrong things
but the feeling wears off . . .

How do you feel? Angry? Lonely? Worthless?
Or just mixed up? Perhaps you're happy or
excited – or even in love!

Gordon Bailey has put together some prayers
which show us something dynamic – that we can tell
God exactly how we feel. We don't need to be
long-winded. And there's certainly no point in
pretending. We simply need to put our feelings
into words and share them with God. He not only
understands us fully – he can actually do something
to help.

'When God sees that we are waiting expectantly
for an answer, he will *always* respond, though not
always as we expect. Be prepared to be surprised
– and you will be.'

Gordon Bailey is a freelance writer and journalist
and has had four books of poetry published. He is
also the compiler of *100 Contemporary Christian
Poets* published by Lion in 1983.

# Contents

A few thoughts about prayer

# A few thoughts about prayer

I talk to my children and they talk to me. We talk together! This is just one way in which we show we belong to one another, that we are a family. Jesus encourages us to talk to God as we would talk to a father we love and respect. The first few words of *The Lord's Prayer* could be put like this: 'Heavenly Father, we respect you very much, we love even the sound of your name.'

I used to think, *if God knows everything I'm thinking why do I need to pray at all?* Then I realized that I enjoyed hearing my children telling me that they love me. I know they do, but it's great to hear them say it. In the same way, God enjoys it when we worship him, when we tell him we love him.

When we are honest with God, telling him how we really feel; when we say 'Thank you' for the things we appreciate; when we are quiet, willing to hear God speaking to us, willing to do whatever he asks; then we are taking part in worship.

We have to pray with faith, and believe God hears and will answer us. God is the most perfect Father, so he always listens and always replies, even if his reply is 'No' or 'Later'.

One young person asked me, 'When should I pray?' *Should* is the wrong word. God does not force his children to talk to him – what would be the point of that? We can pray whenever we want to, or need to: in any circumstances, at any time, and whatever is going on around us. Jesus said that it will sometimes be necessary to shut ourselves away in a quiet room if we are not to be distracted, but, wherever we are, God is ready to have a conversation with us.

My children talk with me in their everyday language, using their normal voice. They do not have special 'Talking to Dad times'. They talk to me at all sorts of times: at meals, when we're out in the car together, on holidays, when we're watching television. Though they have no special times, they do talk to me every day.

We can be very glad that we are able to pray. Think of it: ordinary people like us talking with the God who created everything which is good and beautiful. Fantastic!

In this book are some prayers for you to use on your own. Prayer is mainly a private thing; Jesus said so. But sometimes, as in a human family, God's family will want to pray together as brothers and sisters.

I hope these prayers will help you to begin to tell God how you feel. Read each prayer through before you pray, think about the words, find a prayer which fits in with how you are feeling. Be thoughtful when you pray. Give yourself time. Sit quietly afterwards waiting for God to answer, perhaps reading a few verses in one of the gospels of the new Testament, or go to spend time with someone you know to be a Christian. I say this because God often uses other people to help us, and he also speaks to us by the Holy Spirit as we read the Bible.

When God sees that we are waiting expectantly for an answer, he will always respond, though not always as we expect. Be prepared to be surprised − and you will be.

Gordon Bailey

# I'm glad I can talk to you like this

Dear God,
I heard my friend talking to you
just as if you're real,
just as if you're right here with us.
Now I'm talking to you.
I'm glad I can talk to you like this,
ordinary like, no fuss,
like chatting with a friend, or one of the family,
somebody I love.
It's more like a conversation,
which means, I suppose,
that, as well as talking to you I can listen,
just sit here, quiet,
and expect you to say something;
you speaking to me through my own thoughts,
or someone else's words,
or the trees outside the window.
Help me to understand you,
please.

I'm tongue-tied

I'm finding it hard to pray, God;
I never know what to say.
Well, all right, *sometimes* I don't know what to say.
I don't think I'm afraid of you,
or embarrassed by you,
or short of things to talk about;
I think it's because I'm just not used to praying.
Maybe, because, for me,
praying seems such an odd thing to do,
I'm tongue-tied.
Can you help me, please?

I'm excited


I feel like something good is going to happen God:
either to me, which would be great,
or to someone who is precious to me,
and that'd be great as well.

Even if nothing out-of-the-ordinary happens
I just want to say 'Thank you'
for the ordinary,
for just being alive,
and for this feeling of excitement.
It's good!
Thank you.

## I'm afraid

You know what I'm scared of, don't you Jesus?
I try to pretend I'm brave,
but you know better.
So do I.
Why am I scared of being scared?

I heard somewhere that fear is good, it's necessary:
if we couldn't feel fear we'd make all sorts
        of terrible mistakes;
but still, I don't feel glad or grateful
        when my fears come –
I just feel all tight inside.

Perhaps, Jesus, if you helped me
to look forward to good things
instead of being afraid of the bad
maybe then I would feel better.
Does that make sense?

I'm happy

I've had a good day, God.
Even this morning turned out better than I'd expected.
Now I'm feeling happy.
Help me to enjoy this good feeling
and learn to make it last,
because I've noticed how people I'm with can share
my happiness,
it sort of spreads itself around.
Thank you.

I'm sad


Oh Lord Jesus
I feel sad, miserable, downright unhappy.
You must have felt the same
when your friends betrayed you;
when people you had helped took you for granted,
and couldn't even be bothered to say 'Thank you';
so you must be able to understand how I feel.
Now there's a thought:
my sadness might help me
to understand my friends when they feel miserable.
Thanks, Jesus,
I feel a bit better already.

# I'm grateful

I want to say
'Thank you, God!'
Thanks for being there,
thanks for listening,
thanks for having time for me,
thanks for all the good in the world:
good people, good things, good places;
if I can help at all,
with some of the not-so-good things,
here I am Lord –
grateful.

I feel rotten

O God, I feel rotten.
You know what I did,
and you know how lousy it's making me feel;
I didn't think I had much of a conscience,
till now.
You'd think feelings as bad as this would stop me
doing wrong things
but the feeling wears off . . .
perhaps God, if I could understand *why*
certain things are wrong,
and not just 'because you say so',
maybe then I'd want to be different,
I don't know.
But I want to stop feeling rotten.
I'm sorry.

# I'm pleased

Some people might call me 'smug', Jesus,
but you know I'm not;
I'm just pleased.
I found pleasure in something,
it was beautiful,
I'd never seen anything like it;
I was given enjoyment by someone,
just being with them was good,
getting to know them,
listening to them,
watching them,
seeing who they were.
They seemed to enjoy being with me;
we were pleased to be together.
I still feel pleased,
thinking about them.
Thank you.

I've just realized how valuable friends are

Jesus, it never dawned on me before,
not like this anyway –
that friends are precious.
Thank you for letting me see
how much my friends mean to me.
Help me to be a friend
who can be relied upon.
Amen.

I'm worried


I'm not exactly afraid of the future, God,
but I am worried.
I worry about all kinds of things.
Sometimes I worry about being worried!
Perhaps,
if I really believed you are in charge of things,
even though it doesn't look like it sometimes,
perhaps then I wouldn't worry so much.
Maybe I need to believe in you more:
more truly, more deeply, more often.
I do trust you, Lord,
but please help me
to trust you more.

## I'm all agog

Your world, your creation, God,
it's mind-blowing!
Variety, beauty, colour, contrasts:
unique snowflakes which melt on my fingers,
mountains more than five miles high,
oceans and icicles,
forests and fir-cones,
deserts and . . . er, egg-timers.
Your universe, God,
I'm all agog!
From the invisible to the unimaginable,
and, amongst all this,
me,
and my family, and my friends,
and people like me all over the world.
For the fact that everywhere there is something good,
thank you, God.

I'm lonely


Lord, I'm finding myself hard to understand:
see, there are nearly four billion people
crammed onto this planet, and yet,
somehow or other, I feel lonely!
You must have felt lonely
when you said your Father had left you,
you know, when you were dying.
Jesus, never let me be *that* lonely, please;
I couldn't bear it, not like you did.
Daft as it might seem, with all these people about,
I do feel lonely.
I'm just telling you honestly how I feel.
So, please help me, Jesus,
I need you as a friend.

# I'm angry

I feel angry, God.
I know it's all right to feel worked up
about injustice, and war,
and terrorism and so on,
and I do care about all those things;
but, right now, I'm seething, boiling,
hopping mad – I'm furious!
And you know why?
Somewhere inside me someone lit a fuse
and, unless you help me,
I'm going to go off with a very loud bang.
Calm me down, Lord;
help me sort out my feelings;
help me to be more like Jesus:
he stayed calm when all sorts of terrible things
were done to him,
when awful things were said about him;
help me to believe in you.
I need you.

I'm bored

God,
is it true
that boredom is a belly-rumble of a hungry mind?
If so, then my mind isn't rumbling,
it's erupting!
I'm bored, really, really bored.
They say we're in for even more unemployment,
more leisure time,
so it's going to get worse, this boredom.
I do things when I'm bored
that I'm sorry for later on;
I make others feel miserable as well.
Please help me to learn
how to care for and feed my mind,
how to keep it completely satisfied.
Will you?

I feel all nice inside

It's nothing I could pin down, Lord,
or put my finger on,
just this sort of warm glow inside somewhere,
a nice, secure feeling, safe . . .
I'd like everyone to feel like this.
Could I share this feeling?
Please, God,
do help me.

# I'm hanging back

You hesitated once, Jesus,
as death approached,
and you wondered over possibilities.
I'm hanging back,
hesitant, afraid, unsure.
I need your help, Lord,
as I make up my mind,
because I want to do right.
Right is what you want me to do,
so please
help me.

I feel optimistic


I've heard people talk about things
getting worse –
wars, the weather, the whole world –
but I actually feel hopeful.

Maybe it's because it is a fact that
light always chases darkness away:
by the sun's rising,
by a candle's gleaming,
by the flick of a switch,
and without fail when there is power.
Lord, you *are* power,
you are light;
the Light of the world;
and you never fail.
You give me hope.
Thank you.

You amaze me

You're incredible, Lord,
fantastic!
So great, so mind-boggling,
so far beyond understanding, and yet
you came to earth as a baby,
grew to be a man,
but more than just a man,
no mere man could be as great as you are.
And then,
you who can never die chose to submit to death
for the best and the worst in me:
to encourage the best
and transform the worst.
You amaze me, you make me wonder;
and you have given me the gift of faith
which makes the unbelievable believable.
Thank you.

I feel as if I'm losing my faith

These doubts and uncertainties
are bothering me, Jesus.
One minute I can't help but believe in you,
the next minute I *need* help to believe in you.
You made faith, right?
Together with everything that is good?
Well, I need a bit,
now;
and I need to be made willing to use it.

Please help me, Jesus.

I feel like I love you

Jesus –
the very thought of you turns me on.
But more than that:
I am attracted to you;
but more than that:
I like you;
but more than that:
I enjoy your friendship;
but more than that:
I am grateful to you;
but more than that,
far more:
I love you, Lord Jesus,
I love you as completely as I am able to,
and more than that . . .

Everybody's against me


I feel as if nobody loves me.
Honest to God, that's how I feel, Jesus.
I'm told you love me always, for ever,
that my parents love me,
but that's not how I feel.
I'm hurting inside.
I feel alone, lost, on my own:
that's how I feel.

I suppose I know you love me,
and so do other people,
but, right now,
my feeling doesn't match my knowing;
oh, I don't know what I feel!
To say
'Everybody is against me'
is an exaggeration, but
it is how I feel.
I think.
Please help me.

I think I'm in love


If it's true that you feel love, God,
love towards everything you have made,
then, Lord, perhaps you know
how I'm feeling,
only more so.
I feel high, tingly, excited.
I think I'm in love.

Have you brought us together, God?
Are we right for one another?
Can it possibly last a lifetime?
Is it too good to be true?
Am I asking the right questions?

Help me to understand what is happening;
help me not to depend too much on feelings
(though I thank you for them, I feel good!);
help me to distinguish truth from fantasy,
you know I tend to dream a bit;
help me not to shut you out of this new relationship;
we're going to need you.
You *are* love.

I'm all mixed up


So many pressures on me, God,
pushing this way and that,
threatening to tear me apart;
that's how I feel.

Teachers, parents, friends,
magazines, television, advertising,
ambition, impatience, frustration,
they get me all tied up inside,
good and evil staging a tug-of-war in my mind.

Help me to see tension positively:
stress exercises and strengthens muscles.
Help me to grow stronger through pressure,
save me from giving in when I should be going on.

I feel all mixed up, Lord,
I need sorting out,
in my mind.
I need you to sort me out,
and then to go on helping me.

I'm glad we made it up


It was the most awful argument, Lord.
We hurt one another
with words − using words as weapons.
Forgive me, Lord.
I just hit out.
But now
we've made it up.
Thank you.
Not so long ago
I would have carried on the conflict,
the fight would've lasted longer,
till I thought I'd won, or
till I had the last word.
Thank you for helping me to control my tongue.
It seems I'll always need you.

I feel worthless

Why do you care about me?
I'm not worth it.
I'm rotten.
I can't seem to do the right thing, ever.
Why should anyone love me,
especially you, Lord?
I feel worthless.

Yet –
my mind keeps coming back to you.
(That's probably why I'm praying.)

If human beings were perfect
we wouldn't need you.
You said you came to earth to live and die
for sinners.
Well, I'm definitely a sinner.
If that gives me some value in your eyes, Lord,
thank you.
I can't understand that,
but I really want to believe it.

I feel great


Jesus, I feel great,
just great!
I may not feel like this tomorrow,
but I just wanted to let you know
that I'm glad I feel great today.
Thank you, Jesus.

I'm fed up


I'm fed up, God,
fed up to the back teeth.
I'm cheesed off.

I'm sorry to say it
but it's the truth.
You know what it's all about, so
you shouldn't be surprised, Lord.

If you have the answer
I'm asking the question;
speak to me.

I feel relieved


It wasn't as bad as I thought it would be.
I worried for nothing, didn't I?
I feel so relieved.
Thank you, Lord.

Am I too much of a pessimist?
Whatever . . .
I feel good now.

Sure, it wasn't a barrel of laughs,
but it was nowhere near as bad as I'd feared.
I'm sure there must be something to learn,
something about trusting you.
Be my teacher, Lord.

I feel as if nothing could move me

I feel as if nothing could move me;
as if my roots went down a million miles
through solid rock;
as if I could withstand anything.

Is it stupid or dangerous to feel as secure as this?
Is it asking for trouble?
What if it is.
What if the worst happened.
I know where my roots are –
in you, Lord!
I trust you.
But the problem
is that I become self-confident,
and then, ask for it or not,
I get trouble;
and my security evaporates.

If I keep on trusting in you,
nothing can move me.
Thank you, Lord,
for being such a sure foundation.

I'm heartbroken

It's all gone wrong, Lord,
the bottom has fallen out of my world.
I'm heartbroken.

Just yesterday my heart was full of love,
of faith, of hope,
but then my heart was broken
and its contents spilled out.
I feel utterly empty.

How could you deliberately empty yourself, Jesus?
They say that
when your heart was broken
blood and water poured out.
I've thought about that:
blood gives life and water gives health;
well, my life needs healing.
Can you heal broken hearts, Jesus?
I need you.

I'm over the moon!


It all went so very well, Lord:
the planning,
the preparation,
the doing it,
the success.
I'm over the moon!
I can hardly believe it's happened.

Mind you,
I can't take all the credit, can I?
I did ask for your help.
Maybe I shouldn't take *any* of the credit.
Thank you, God.

## I'm desperate

I feel desperate, Lord,
as if I might do something really stupid.
I'm at my wits' end.
I've racked my brains,
I've tried all sorts of ways out of this situation,
but I keep on coming up against dead-ends.
I'm desperate, Lord.

I know I can't be the only one who's ever felt
        like this,
but, right now, I feel dreadful.
You're my last chance, Lord,
my only hope.
Help me, please.

I'm frustrated


It almost came off, Lord,
I nearly made it.
If I'd missed by a mile
I wouldn't be feeling so frustrated,
but it nearly came off.
A gnat's whisker away, that's all,
a termite's sneeze!
And, as usual, I was told,
'Never count your chickens'.

What have I learned, Lord,
what can you teach me?
To keep on trying?
To be willing to fail?
To learn from mistakes,
including being over-confident?
To think positively?
To put into practice the faith I claim to possess?

Thank you, Lord,
thank you for making enough time for us to learn.

I'm dead beat

Lord, I'm dead beat,
shattered, popped, absolutely crankimated!

I could've taken the day off,
left it all to somebody else,
and I do know I'm not indispensable,
but I did it all myself, Lord,
and I'm tired out.

Mind you,
I'm not complaining.
It's a nice sort of feeling:
a pleasant, job-well-done sort of weariness.

Thank you for giving us sleep.
Refresh me, Lord.

## I'm satisfied

You make me feel good, Lord,
and I'm satisfied.

I've noticed you and appreciated you
in love between people,
in loyalty amongst friends,
in kindness, in care, in concern, in compassion.

I tend to get caught up in the bad news,
the headlines in the papers,
and, when I do, I don't see you any more.

Bad news gets us all down, Lord,
it's depressing.
Help us to do something about it,
to create more good news,
to tip the scales the other way.
If you want to use me as you answer this prayer,
here I am, God,
use me.
And thank you for satisfying me.

# I feel relaxed

I used to be a tense sort of person, God,
but you showed me how to trust you.
Now,
I'm learning to let you take the strain,
I am learning to unwind.
I feel relaxed.
It's a good feeling.
Thank you, Lord.

# It hurts, Lord

I didn't know pain could be as bad as this.
Oh,
it hurts, Lord.
A teacher said 'Pain is good,
it's the body's warning signal.'
I don't feel good!
Why is my body shouting at me like this?
What have I done?
Or not done?
Do I need to put a higher value on health?
Take more care of my body?

I believe you made the human body, Lord,
made it good.
Can you make good out of my body,
even though I've neglected it?

Show me how to respect what you have made,
teach me to learn from this pain, Lord.
Forgive me.

## I feel better

I didn't enjoy being under the weather, God,
but I feel better now.
Thank you.
Teach me how to help others
who suffer, and
thank you for those who were good to me,
who helped me to feel better.

Help me never to forget
that there are people around me
who will never feel better;
help me to help them feel good.
Thinking of others doesn't come easy, Lord,
so I'll need you.

It's not fair!


Life can be so grotty.
It can kick you in the kidneys
when you least expect it.
You see, God,
I can't think of anything I've done to deserve this,
this feeling that life is treating me badly
without reason.
It's not fair!
It's unjust.
If I could come up with some explanation . . .
but I can't, honestly.

Yes, I know,
there are other people much worse off than me,
but that doesn't help.

I need you.
This is one of those times when
I just don't know what to do.
The more I try to work it out
the worse I feel.
Please help me.

## Living's fantastic!

It's as if my eyes can see only good things;
as if life is suddenly keeping all its promises;
as if evil has been obliterated.
Oh yes,
I know it hasn't,
that I'll probably come down to earth with a dull
      krump,
that I might wake up in a minute with brainache,
but,
right now,
it's magic!

Life's a funny old mixture.

I know it can't always be like this,
but, for this experience of feeling great,
thank you, God.
It's fantastic!

I love a good argument


I'm wicked, really, Lord.
It isn't even that I hate people,
or even dislike them,
I just love a good argument.
I enjoy the heat it generates.
I can warm myself at the fire;
the flames of conflict lick at my mind
        and I feel good.

I'm not even serious,
I'm smiling inside, especially when the other person
gets more and more angry.

My conscience does bother me sometimes,
but I tend not to listen until it's too late,
and there are tears or, worse,
a broken relationship.

I'm sure you don't like me being like this, God,
and, sometimes, I wish I wasn't like it.
Could you strengthen the wish,
fulfil the desire?
I need you.

## Nothing matters

I'm in one of those couldn't-care-less moods, God.
I'm sorry.
That's just how I feel:
as if nothing matters.
I expect you might feel insulted
when I feel like this
but it happens from time to time.
Why?
Is it the same for everyone?
All sorts of words and phrases describe the way I feel:
indifference, apathy, disinterest,
and, come to think of it,
it is as if I actually feel nothing.
I'm sort of numb inside.

Wake me, Lord,
shake me up,
startle me.
You have so much at your elbow, God,
so many amazing things,
you ought to find it easy to disturb me,
to break this negative, destructive mood.

Being honest though
I'm not sure I want disturbing.
Help me.

I matter

You make me feel important, God,
you have shown me that,
so far as you are concerned,
I matter.

I matter so much to you
that you allowed Jesus to be put to death
for my sake.

That just amazes me
and I don't really understand love like that,
it's beyond me.

Feeling *that* important is good.
Thank you for the value you place upon me.

Would it be possible for me to see things
through your eyes?
If I could I'd most likely value my family
and my friends more highly.
Help me to love people like you do, or,
if that isn't possible,
help me to love them
more than I do now.
Please.

# I'd like to be a peacemaker

I sense a craving in the world, Jesus,
a hunger for peace.
I share this feeling.
It makes me want to march, sometimes,
to join one of the peace movements,
but then I hesitate and I don't know why.

I feel strongly about it:
there ought not to be wars;
it's wrong for more to be spent on weapons
than on medical research;
those with power do seem to abuse it,
more often than not;
am I wrong?
I don't mean to be critical of others,
there's aggression and selfishness in me.
Forgive me, Lord.

I cannot imagine how someone as insignificant as me
could ever influence anyone towards peace,
but if, with your help, such a thing is possible,
help me, Lord,
help me.
I'd like to be a peacemaker.

# I'm jealous

I'm jealous,
emerald green with resentment.
Why that person and not me?
You know what I'm talking about, Jesus,
you know exactly.

Forgive me,
I can't help it.

A great many things around me actually encourage
    envy.
Phoney standards are drawn for me,
my attention is drawn to them over and over again;
it tends to be those who are after my money
and, even though I know what they're up to,
their lies are so very clever
and sound like truths.

Jealousy is so silly, Lord,
but knowing that doesn't stop me feeling it.
Be my distraction, Jesus,
win the battle for my eyes and ears and mind.
Jesus, please help me,
jealousy can be so destructive.

I'm too well off


I have this guilt-feeling, Lord,
every time I see pictures from the third world.
I'm too well-off.
I thought I was hard done by
until I saw the poverty in parts of Africa
        and South America.
Forgive me, Lord.

My guilt may be unnecessary,
I don't know,
but I'm sure that me feeling guilty won't achieve much,
not if I just feel *guilty*.
I need to feel compassion, Lord,
I need to believe that I can do something to help,
I need to let go of my personal ambition,
I need to be fully committed to you and what you want.

You want hunger relieved, don't you, Lord?
You want resources to be shared out properly, right?
You want people like me to be willing to serve others,
I know that's what you want.

I think I would be of help
if I wanted what you want.
Help me, Lord.

I'm lazy

I don't have to tell you, Lord,
I'm lazy:
active as a fossil, I am!

I have trouble with my feet –
they prefer slippers to walking shoes!

Forgive me, Jesus.
You sweated blood for me.
You ask me to follow you but I prefer my comfort;
you place opportunities before me but I bury my head
in my pillow;
you encourage me from within, putting thoughts
        in my mind,
but I nod off.
Teach me, Lord, the folly of idleness,
that it hardens the arteries of a loving heart.

I'm praying, Lord, because, deep down,
I don't want to go on being lazy.
Change me.

I feel as if I could change the world

I have this sensation of power, God,
as if . . .
as if I don't really need you.

I feel as if *I* could change the world.
If only I could be in the right place
at the right time;
if only I could write the front page of *The Times*;
if only I could be given an hour
        on worldwide television;
if only I was a millionaire;
if I ruled the world!

I expect that Hitler and the Caesars felt like this.

It's wrong isn't it, Lord?
After all, it is your world, not ours.
We need you.
You have a plan, a design, a purpose for your world,
and we get in your way don't we?
*I* get in your way,
with my ambitions which differ from what you want,
with my selfishness and greed,
with my feeling of power.

God, you are Lord.
Help me fit in with your plans.
Keep me trusting you.

I get confused

So many voices, Jesus,
all claiming to have the solutions to life's problems.
I get confused.

There are sensible voices,
religious voices,
persuasive voices,
political voices,
everywhere, Lord, on radio and television,
in newspapers and magazines,
different voices.
Help me, Lord, to tell the difference
between what makes sense and what is right,
between what is 'good' and what is God.

I just thought of something funny,
I hope you don't mind –
GOOD is GOD with nothing added!
Or GOD is GOOD with nothing taken away.
It's not funny, is it? But it's right,
it's true.
Help me to want all of you, Lord,
nothing taken away;
help me to see you like that;
that'd be the beginning of the end of my confusion.
Help me to hear your voice.

I see

Thank you, Jesus,
thanks ever so much.
I asked you to help me and you have done.

It was confusing for a while,
I was all mixed up,
but you have opened my eyes;
I see!
I didn't know how to see good with so much evil about;
I didn't know how to see your way,
        so obsessed was I with mine.
You have expanded my horizon,
you have extended my vision,
you have added colour and shape and beauty and light.
For the ability to see
thank you, Lord.

I don't know what to do


I have a decision to make, Jesus,
and I don't know what to do.
If it was black and white it wouldn't be a problem,
well, not *understanding* what to do; though
actually *doing* it might be difficult.
Just now I'm trying to sort out the first bit:
right from wrong, or even
right from right.

I'm glad I have the chance to choose,
it is a luxury,
but I do need help with the choosing.
It would help me, Lord,
if you would make it clear to me –
what *you* want.
Will you?
Please.

I'm sorry


You know what I've done,
Lord God,
and, no doubt, you're reminding me
that I need your help in putting the wrong thing right.
I'm sorry.
Please forgive me.
Help me not to do the same thing again.

I expect you want me to apologise for what I've done.
That'll be hard.

So, Lord, as well as your forgiveness,
I need your help
and encouragement,
until I've done what's right.

I feel as if I belong to you


Since first I asked your forgiveness, Lord,
and since I asked you to come into my life,
I have a deep-down sense of belonging.
I feel accepted;
accepted by you.
Yes, by you, and that's great!

I also feel accepted by other people,
the rest of your family,
and that's great too.
Thank you for all my new brothers and sisters.

Being accepted into your family,
by you and them,
is going to make a big difference in my life.
Thank you.

## Thank God

I hugged someone today and the world's coldness for a moment disappeared. Why don't I do it more often?

'This is a book of meditations, thoughts. . . The setting is the world, life, living. That means war, unemployment, racism, ecology. That means falling in love, parents, clothes, bed-sits . . . TV, records, music. *Thank God* is about me, you. . .

'This book springs off one major belief: Jesus *is*. Jesus is the one person who tells us about God. He breaks through and makes sense of ourselves. . . So let's thank God for Jesus — here and now!'

Tony Jasper has written thirty books: on rock music, on the Christian faith, and books for schools. He has several weekly radio programmes and works as a rock journalist. He is also an active Methodist local preacher. He comes from Penzance, Cornwall and lives in London.

# Home-made Prayers

'Do you ever pray?'

A strange question for today – but Janet Green was
amazed at the response. Two-thirds of the comprehensive
school where she teaches admitted to saying prayers
fairly often. And they didn't mind talking about it.

'In the first class I approached, a second year told
me that he had prayed yesterday. Yesterday being
Sunday, I asked if he went to church.

' "No," he said, "I went rabbiting."
' "What sort of prayers do you say when you go rabbiting?"
' "Please God let my ferret come out."

'We didn't reckon much to it as a prayer but it
raised interesting questions. What happens if the
ferret doesn't come out? And what if it does?
Next time that happens, he says he's going to
remember to say thank you.'

Illustrated by photographs taken by the teenagers
themselves, *Home-made Prayers* is a collection of
refreshingly honest conversations with God – some
more urgent than others!

Janet Green has written a number of books
for schools and worked on a television
series for the B.B.C. She is currently
Head of R.E. and Drama at Greenway Boys'
School in Bristol.

# I WANT TO TELL YOU HOW I FEEL, GOD

'O God, I feel rotten.
You know what I did,
and you know
how lousy it's making me feel;
I didn't think I had much of a conscience, till now.
You'd think feelings as bad as this would stop me
doing wrong things but the feeling wears off...'

How do you feel?
Angry? Lonely? Worthless? Or just mixed up?
Perhaps you're happy or excited — or even in love!

Gordon Bailey has put together some prayers
which show us something dynamic — that we can tell God
exactly how we feel. We don't need to be long-winded.
And there's certainly no point in pretending.
We simply need to put our feelings into words
and share them with God. He not only understands
us fully — he can actually do something to help.

'When God sees
that we are waiting expectantly for an answer,
he will always respond, though not always as we expect.
Be prepared to be surprised — and you will be.'

ISBN 0-85648-339-7

A LION
PAPERBACK

UK          £1.50
Australia *$3.95
ISBN 0 86760 385 2
*Recommended price

9 780856 483394